The BAPTISM AND CONFIRMATION BOOK

The BAPTISM AND CONFIRMATION BOOK

EBURY PRESS
LONDON

First published 1993
1 3 5 7 9 10 8 6 4 2

First published in the United Kingdom in 1993 by
Ebury Press Limited
Random House, 20 Vauxhall Bridge Road,
London SW1V 2SA

Random House Australia (Pty) Limited
20 Alfred Street, Milsons Point, Sydney,
New South Wales 2061, Australia

Random House New Zealand Limited
18 Poland Road, Glenfield
Auckland 10, New Zealand

Random House South Africa (Pty) Limited
PO Box 337, Bergvlei, South Africa

Random House YK Limited Reg. No 954009
Design by David Fordham
Picture research by Philippa Lewis

A CIP catalogue record for this book
is available from the British Library
ISBN 0 09 177876 X

Printed in Great Britain by
Typeset by SX Composing Limited, Rayleigh, Essex

CONTENTS

THE PUBLIC BAPTISM OF INFANTS
FROM THE BOOK OF COMMON PRAYER..............7

THE BAPTISM OF CHILDREN FROM THE
ALTERNATIVE SERVICE BOOK 21

THE RITE OF BAPTISM FOR CHILDREN
IN THE CATHOLIC CHURCH..........................33

THE ORDER OF CONFIRMATION 55

THE CONFIRMATION IN THE ALTERNATIVE
VERSION...61

CONFIRMATION OUTSIDE MASS 75

PICTURE CREDITS.......................................96

ACKNOWLEDGEMENTS

The Public Baptism of Infants from *The Book of Common Prayer*, the rights in which are vested in the Crown, are reproduced by permission of the Crown Patentee, Cambridge University Press.

The Baptism of Children from *The Alternative Service Book 1980*, copyright © The Central Board of Finance of the Church of England, is reproduced with permission.

The Rite of Baptism for Children outside Mass in the Catholic Church: Excerpts from the English translation of *Rite of Baptism for Children* © 1969, International Committee on English in the Liturgy, Inc. (ICEL). All rights reserved.

The MINISTRATION of PUBLICK BAPTISM of INFANTS from The BOOK of COMMON PRAYER

TO BE USED IN THE CHURCH

Due notice, normally of at least a week, shall be given before a child is brought to the church to be baptized. For every child to be baptized there shall be not fewer than three godparents, of whom at least two shall be of the same sex as the child and of whom at least one shall be of the opposite sex; save that, when three cannot be conveniently had, one godfather and one godmother shall suffice. Parents may be godparents for their own children provided that the child shall have at least one other godparent. The godparents shall be persons who have been baptized and confirmed and will faithfully fulfil their responsibilities both by their care for the child committed to their charge and by the example of their own godly living. Nevertheless the Minister shall have power to dispense with the requirement of confirmation in any case in which in his judgement need so requires. The Minister shall instruct the parents or guardians of an infant to be admitted to Holy Baptism that the same responsibilities rest on them as are in the service of Holy Baptism required of the godparents.

No Minister shall refuse or, save for the purpose of preparing or instructing the parents or guardians or godparents, delay to baptize any infant within his cure that is brought to the church to be baptized, provided that due notice has been given and the provisions relating to godparents are observed. If the Minister shall refuse or unduly delay to baptize any such infant, the parents or guardians may apply to the Bishop of the diocese who shall, after consultation with the Minister, give such directions as he thinks fit.
The Minister, before proceeding to the Baptism, shall have satisfied himself that the child presented to him has not already been baptized.
At the time appointed the godfathers and godmothers and the parents or guardians with the child must be ready at the Font, and the Priest coming to the Font (which is then to be filled with pure Water), and standing there, shall say:

DEARLY beloved, forasmuch as all men are conceived and born in sin: and that our Saviour Christ saith, None can enter into the kingdom of God, except he be regenerate and born anew of Water and of the Holy Ghost: I beseech you to call upon God the Father, through our Lord Jesus Christ, that of his bounteous mercy he will grant to *this Child* that thing which by nature *he* cannot have; that *he* may be baptized with Water and the Holy Ghost, and received into Christ's holy Church, and be made *a lively member* of the same.

Then shall the Priest say,
Let us pray.

ALMIGHTY and everlasting God, who of thy great mercy didst save Noah and his family in the ark from perishing by water; and also didst safely lead the children of Israel thy people through the Red Sea, figuring thereby thy holy Baptism; and by the Baptism of thy well-beloved Son Jesus Christ, in the river Jordan, didst sanctify Water to the mystical washing away of sin: We beseech thee, for thine infinite mercies, that thou wilt mercifully look upon *this Child*; wash *him* and sanctify *him* with the Holy Ghost; that *he*, being delivered from thy wrath, may be received into the ark of Christ's Church; and being stedfast in faith, joyful through hope, and rooted in charity, may so pass the waves of this troublesome world, that finally *he* may come to the land of everlasting life, there to reign with thee world without end; through Jesus Christ our Lord. *Amen.*

ALMIGHTY and immortal God, the aid of all that need, the helper of all that flee to thee for succour, the life of them that believe, and the resurrection of the dead: We call upon thee for *this Infant*, that *he*, coming to thy holy Baptism, may receive remission of *his* sins by spiritual regeneration. Receive *him*, O Lord, as thou hast promised by thy well-beloved Son, saying, Ask, and ye shall have; seek, and ye shall find; knock, and it shall be opened unto you: So give now unto us that ask; let us that seek find; open the gate unto us that knock; that *this Infant* may enjoy the everlasting benediction of thy heavenly washing, and may come to the eternal kingdom which thou hast promised by Christ our Lord. *Amen.*

Then shall the people stand up, and the Priest shall say,

HEAR the words of the Gospel, written by Saint *Mark*, in the tenth Chapter, at the thirteenth Verse.

THEY brought young children to Christ, that he should touch them; and his disciples rebuked those that brought them. But when Jesus saw it, he was much displeased, and said unto them, Suffer the little children to come unto me, and forbid them not; for of such is the kingdom of God. Verily I say unto you, Whosoever shall not receive the kingdom of God as a little child, he shall not enter therein. And he took them up in his arms, put his hands upon them, and blessed them.

After the Gospel is read, the Minister shall make this brief Exhortation upon the words of the Gospel.

BELOVED, ye hear in this Gospel the words of our Saviour Christ, that he commanded the children to be brought unto him; how he blamed those that would have kept them from him; how he exhorteth all men to follow their innocency. Ye perceive how by his outward gesture and deed he declared his good will toward them; for he embraced them in his arms, he laid his hands upon them, and blessed them. Doubt ye not therefore, but earnestly believe, that he will likewise favourably receive *this* present *Infant*; that he will embrace *him* with the arms of his mercy; that he will give unto *him* the blessing of eternal life, and make *him partaker* of his everlasting kingdom. Wherefore we being thus persuaded of the good will of our heavenly Father towards *this Infant*, declared by his Son Jesus Christ; and nothing doubting but that he favourably alloweth this charitable work of ours in bringing *this Infant* to his holy Baptism; let us faithfully and devoutly give thanks unto him, and say,

ALMIGHTY and everlasting God, heavenly Father, we give thee humble thanks, for that thou hast vouchsafed to call us to the knowledge of thy grace, and faith in thee: Increase this knowledge, and confirm this faith in us evermore. Give thy Holy Spirit to *this Infant*, that *he* may be born again, and be made *an heir* of everlasting salvation; through our Lord Jesus Christ, who liveth and reigneth with thee and the Holy Spirit, now and for ever. *Amen.*

Then shall the Priest speak unto the Godfathers and Godmothers on this wise.

DEARLY beloved, ye have brought *this Child* here to be baptized, ye have prayed that our Lord Jesus Christ would vouchsafe to receive *him*, to release *him* of *his* sins, to sanctify *him* with the Holy Ghost, to give *him* the kingdom of heaven, and everlasting life. Ye have heard also that our Lord Jesus Christ hath promised in his Gospel to grant all these things that ye have prayed for: which promise he, for his part, will most surely keep and perform. Wherefore, after this promise made by Christ, *this Infant* must also faithfully, for *his* part, promise by you that are *his* sureties, (until *he* come of age to take it upon *himself,*) that *he* will renounce the devil and all his works, and constantly believe God's holy Word, and obediently keep his commandments.

I demand therefore,

Dost thou, in the name of this Child, renounce the devil and all his works, the vain pomp and glory of the world, with all covetous desires of the same, and the carnal desires of the flesh, so that thou wilt not follow, nor be led by them?

Answer. I renounce them all.

Minister.

Dost thou believe in God the Father Almighty, Maker of heaven and earth?

And in Jesus Christ his only-begotten Son our Lord? And that he was conceived by the Holy Ghost; born of the Virgin Mary; that he suffered under Pontius Pilate, was crucified, dead, and buried; that he went down into hell, and also did rise again the third day; that he ascended into heaven, and sitteth at the right hand of God the Father Almighty; and from thence shall come again at the end of the world, to judge the quick and the dead?

And dost thou believe in the Holy Ghost; the holy Catholick Church; the Communion of Saints; the Remission of sins; the Resurrection of the flesh; and everlasting life after death?

Answer. All this I stedfastly believe.

✤

Minister.
Wilt thou be baptized in this faith?

✤

Answer. That is my desire.

✤

Minister.
WILT thou then obediently keep God's holy will and commandments, and walk in the same all the days of thy life?

✤

Answer. I will.

Then shall the Priest say,

O MERCIFUL God, grant that the old Adam in *this Child* may be so buried, that the new man may be raised up in *him.* Amen.

Grant that all carnal affections may die in *him,* and that all things belonging to the Spirit may live and grow in *him.* Amen.

Grant that *he* may have power and strength to have victory, and to triumph, against the devil, the world, and the flesh. *Amen.*

Grant that whosoever is here dedicated to thee by our office and ministry may also be endued with heavenly virtues, and everlastingly rewarded, through thy mercy, O blessed Lord God, who dost live, and govern all things, world without end. *Amen.*

ALMIGHTY, everliving God, whose most dearly beloved Son Jesus Christ, for the forgiveness of our sins, did shed out of his most precious side both water and blood; and gave commandment to his disciples, that they should go teach all nations, and baptize them In the Name of the Father, and of the Son, and of the Holy Ghost: Regard, we beseech thee, the supplications of thy congregation; sanctify this Water to the mystical washing away of sin; and grant that *this Child,* now to be baptized therein, may receive the fulness of thy grace, and ever remain in the number of thy faithful and elect children; through Jesus Christ our Lord. *Amen.*

Then the Priest shall take the Child into his hands, and shall say to the Godfathers and Godmothers,

Name this Child.

And then naming it after them (if they shall certify him that the Child may well endure it) he shall dip it in the Water discreetly and warily, saying,

N. I BAPTIZE thee In the Name of the Father, and of the Son, and of the Holy Ghost. Amen.

But if they certify that the Child is weak, it shall suffice to pour Water upon it, saying the foresaid words,

N. I BAPTIZE thee In the Name of the Father, and of the Son, and of the Holy Ghost. Amen.

Then the Priest shall say,

WE receive this Child into the congregation of Christ's flock, * and do sign *him* with the sign of the Cross, in token that hereafter *he* shall not be ashamed to confess the faith of Christ crucified, and manfully to fight under his banner, against sin, the world, and the devil; and to continue Christ's faithful soldier and servant unto *his* life's end. Amen.

Then shall the Priest say,

SEEING now, dearly beloved brethren, that *this Child is* regenerate, and grafted into the body of Christ's Church, let us give thanks unto Almighty God for these benefits; and with one accord make our prayers unto him, that *this Child* may lead the rest of *his* life according to this beginning.

---

* Here the Priest shall make a Cross upon the Child's forehead.

Then shall be said, all kneeling;

OUR Father, which art in heaven, Hallowed be thy Name. Thy kingdom come. Thy will be done, in earth as it is in heaven. Give us this day our daily bread. And forgive us our trespasses, As we forgive them that trespass against us. And lead us not into temptation; But deliver us from evil. Amen.

Then shall the Priest say,

WE yield thee hearty thanks, most merciful Father, that it hath pleased thee to regenerate *this Infant* with thy Holy Spirit, to receive *him* for thine own *Child* by adoption, and to incorporate *him* into thy holy Church. And humbly we beseech thee to grant, that *he*, being dead unto sin, and living unto righteousness, and being buried with Christ in his death, may crucify the old man, and utterly abolish the whole body of sin; and that, as *he is* made *partaker* of the death of thy Son, *he* may also be *partaker* of his resurrection; so that finally, with the residue of thy holy Church, *he* may be *an inheritor* of thine everlasting kingdom; through Christ our Lord. *Amen.*

Then, all standing up, the Priest shall say to the Godfathers and Godmothers this Exhortation following.

FORASMUCH as *this Child hath* promised by you *his* sureties to renounce the devil and all his works, to believe in God, and to serve him: ye must remember, that it is your parts and duties to see that *this Infant* be taught, so soon as *he* shall be able to learn, what a solemn vow, promise, and profession, *he hath* here made by you. And that *he* may know these things the better, ye shall call upon *him* to hear Sermons; and chiefly ye shall provide, that *he* may learn the Creed, the Lord's Prayer, and the Ten Commandments, in the vulgar tongue, and all other things which a Christian ought to know and believe to his soul's health;

and that *this Child* may be virtuously brought up to lead a godly and a Christian life; remembering always, that Baptism doth represent unto us our profession; which is, to follow the example of our Saviour Christ, and to be made like unto him; that, as he died, and rose again for us, so should we, who are baptized, die from sin, and rise again unto righteousness; continually mortifying all our evil and corrupt affections and daily proceeding in all virtue and godliness of living.

Then shall he add and say,

Ye are to take care that *this Child* be brought to the Bishop to be confirmed by him, so soon as *he* can say the Creed, the Lord's Prayer, and the Ten Commandments, in the vulgar tongue, and be further instructed in the Church-Catechism set forth for that purpose.

It is certain by God's Word, that Children which are baptized, dying before they commit actual sin, are undoubtedly saved.

To take away all scruple concerning the use of the sign of the Cross in Baptism; the true explication thereof, and the just reasons for the retaining of it, may be seen in the XXXth Canon, first published in the Year MDCIV.

The BAPTISM *of* CHILDREN *from* The ALTERNATIVE SERVICE BOOK

1980

THE DUTIES OF PARENTS AND GODPARENTS

42 *The priest says*

CHILDREN who are too young to profess the Christian faith are baptized on the understanding that they are brought up as Christians within the family of the Church.

As they grow up, they need the help and encouragement of that family, so that they learn to be faithful in public worship and private prayer, to live by trust in God, and come to confirmation.

PARENTS and godparents, the *children* whom you have brought for baptism *depend* chiefly on you for the help and encouragement *they need.* Are you willing to give it to *them* by your prayers, by your example, and by your teaching?

Parents and godparents
I am willing.

43 *And if the child is old enough to understand, the priest speaks to him in these or similar words.*

N. WHEN you are baptized, you become *a member* of a new family. God takes you for his own *child*, and all Christian people will be your brothers and sisters.

THE MINISTRY OF THE WORD

Sections 44, 45, and 46 may be omitted when Baptism is administered at Holy Communion or at Morning or Evening Prayer.

44 *Priest*   The Lord is loving to everyone;

All   **and his mercy is over all his works.**

45 *Priest*

God is the creator of all things, and by the birth of children he gives to parents a share in the work and joy of creation. But we who are born of earthly parents need to be born again. For in the Gospel Jesus tells us that unless a man has been born again, he cannot see the Kingdom of God. And so God gives us the way to a second birth, a new creation and life in union with him.

Baptism is the sign and seal of this new birth. In St. Matthew's Gospel we read of the risen Christ commanding his followers to make disciples of all nations and to baptize men everywhere; and in the Acts of the Apostles we read of St Peter preaching in these words: 'Repent and be baptized in the name of Jesus Christ for the forgiveness of sins; and you shall receive the gift of the Holy Spirit. For the promise is to you and your children and to all that are afar off, everyone whom the Lord calls to him.'

In obedience to this same command we ourselves were baptized and now bring *these children* to baptism.

46 *Priest*

We thank God therefore for our baptism to life in Christ, and we pray for *these children (N)* and say together

All:

Heavenly Father, in your love you have called us to know you, led us to trust you, and bound our life with yours. Surround *these children* with your love; protect *them* from evil; fill *them* with your Holy Spirit; and receive *them* into the family of your Church; that *they* may walk with us in the way of Christ and grow in the knowledge of your love. Amen.

THE DECISION

47 *The parents and godparents stand, and the priest says to them*

Those who bring children to be baptized must affirm their allegiance to Christ and their rejection of all that is evil.

It is your duty to bring up *these children* to fight against evil and to follow Christ.

48

THEREFORE I ask these questions which you must answer for yourselves and for *these children*.

> *Priest* Do you turn to Christ?
> *Answer* **I turn to Christ.**
>
> *Priest* Do you repent of your sins?
> *Answer* **I repent of my sins.**
>
> *Priest* Do you renounce evil?
> *Answer* **I renounce evil.**

49 *Either here or at section 56 the priest makes THE SIGN OF THE CROSS on the forehead of each child, saying to each*

I sign you with the cross, the sign of Christ.

After the signing of each or all, he says

Do not be ashamed to confess the faith of Christ crucified.

All

FIGHT valiantly under the banner of Christ against sin, the world, and the devil, and continue his faithful *soldiers* and *servants* to the end of your *lives*.

50 *Priest*

MAY almighty God deliver you from the powers of darkness, and lead you in the light and obedience of Christ. **Amen.**

51 *A HYMN or PSALM may be sung.*

THE BAPTISM

52 *The priest stands before the water of baptism and says*
Praise God who made heaven and earth,

All
who keeps his promise for ever.

Priest

ALMIGHTY God, whose Son Jesus Christ was baptized in the river Jordan: we thank you for the gift of water to cleanse us and revive us; we thank you that through the waters of the Red Sea, you led your people out of slavery to freedom in the promised land; we thank you that through the deep waters of death you brought your Son, and raised him to life in triumph.

Bless this water, that your *servants* who *are* washed in it may be made one with Christ in his death and in his resurrection, to be cleansed and delivered from all sin.

Send your Holy Spirit upon *them* to bring *them* to new birth in the family of your Church, and raise *them* with Christ to full and eternal life.

For all might, majesty, authority, and power are yours, now and for ever. **Amen.**

53 *The priest says to the parents and godparents*

You have brought *these children* to baptism. You must now declare before God and his Church the Christian faith into which *they are* to be baptized, and in which you will help *them* to grow. You must answer for yourselves and for *these children*.

Priest Do you believe and trust in God the Father, who made the world?

Answer **I believe and trust in him.**

Priest Do you believe and trust in his Son Jesus Christ, who redeemed mankind?

Answer **I believe and trust in him.**

Priest Do you believe and trust in his Holy Spirit, who gives life to the people of God?

Answer **I believe and trust in him.**

54 *The priest turns to the congregation and says*

This is the faith of the Church.

All

53 *The priest says to the parents and godparents*

THIS is our faith. We believe and trust in one God, Father, Son, and Holy Spirit.

55 *The parents and godparents being present with each child, the priest baptizes him. He dips him in the water or pours water on him, addressing him by name.*

N. I BAPTIZE you in the name of the Father, and of the Son, and of the Holy Spirit.

And each one of his sponsors answers
Amen.

56 *The priest makes THE SIGN OF THE CROSS on the forehead of each child if he has not already done so. The appropriate words are printed at section 49.*

57 *The priest or other person may give to a parent or godparent for each child A LIGHTED CANDLE, saying to each*

Receive this light.

And when a candle has been given to each one, he says
This is to show that you have passed from darkness to light.

All

Shine as a light in the world to the glory of God the Father.

THE WELCOME

58 *The priest and the congregation, representing the whole Church, welcome the newly baptized.*

Priest
God has received you by baptism into his Church.

All

WE welcome you into the Lord's Family. We are members together of the body of Christ; we are children of the same heavenly Father; we are inheritors together of the kingdom of God. We welcome you.

THE PRAYERS

59 *The prayers that follow are omitted when Baptism is administered at Holy Communion; and may be omitted when Baptism is administered at Morning or Evening Prayer.*

Priest

LORD God our Father, maker of heaven and earth, we thank you that by your Holy Spirit *these children have* been born again into new life, adopted for your own, and received into the fellowship of your Church: grant that *they* may grow in the faith into which *they have* been baptized, that *they* may profess it for *themselves* when *they come* to be confirmed, and that all things belonging to the Spirit may live and grow in *them*. **Amen.**

60 *Priest*

HEAVENLY Father, we pray for the parents of *these children*; give them the spirit of wisdom and love, that their *homes* may reflect the joy of your eternal kingdom. **Amen.**

61 *Priest*

ALMIGHTY God, we thank you for our fellowship in the household of faith with all those who have been baptized in your name. Keep us faithful to our baptism, and so make us ready for that day when the whole creation shall be made perfect in your Son, our Saviour Jesus Christ. **Amen.**

62 *Priest*

JESUS taught us to call God our Father, and so in faith and trust we say

All

OUR Father in heaven, hallowed be your name, your kingdom come, your will be done, on earth as in heaven. Give us today our daily bread. Forgive us our sins as we forgive those who sin against us. Lead us not into temptation but deliver us from evil. For the kingdom, the power, and the glory are yours now and for ever. Amen.

OUR Father, who art in heaven, hallowed be thy name; thy kingdom come; thy will be done; on earth as it is in heaven. Give us this day our daily bread. And forgive us our trespasses, as we forgive those who trespass against us. And lead us not into temptation; but deliver us from evil. For thine is the kingdom, the power, and the glory, for ever and ever. Amen.

63 *Priest*

THE grace of our Lord Jesus Christ, and the love of God, and the fellowship of the Holy Spirit be with us all evermore. **Amen.**

The RITE of BAPTISM for CHILDREN in the CATHOLIC CHURCH

(FOR USE OF THE LAITY)

RECEPTION OF THE CHILD

The people may sing a psalm or hymn while the celebrating priest goes to the entrance of the church or to that part of the church where the parents and godparents are waiting with the child.

The celebrant greets all present. Then he questions the parents:

Celebrant:
What name do you give your child?

Parents: N.

Celebrant:
What do you ask of God's Church for N.?

Parents: **Baptism.**

The celebrant addresses the parents in these or similar words:

You have asked to have your child baptized. In doing so you are accepting the responsibility of training him (her) in the practice of the faith. It will be your duty to bring him (her) up to keep God's commandments as Christ taught us, by loving God and our neighbour. Do you clearly understand what you are undertaking?

Parents: **We do.**

Then the celebrant turns to the godparents:

ARE you ready to help the parents of this child in their duty as Christian parents?

Godparents: **We are.**

Celebrant:

N. THE Christian community welcomes you with great joy. In its name I claim you for Christ our Saviour by the sign of his cross. I now trace the cross on your forehead, and invite your parents (and godparents) to do the same.

He signs the child on the forehead, in silence. Then he invites the parents (and the godparents) to do the same.

CELEBRATION OF GOD'S WORD

One or even two gospel passages are read, during which all may sit.

After the reading the celebrant gives a short homily.

INTERCESSIONS
(The Bidding Prayers)

Celebrant:

My dear brothers and sisters, let us ask our Lord Jesus Christ to look lovingly on this child who is to be baptized, on his (her) parents and godparents, and on all the baptized.

Reader:

By the mystery of your death and resurrection, bathe this child in light, give him (her) the new life of baptism and welcome him (her) into your holy Church. Lord, hear us.

All: **Lord, graciously hear us.**

Reader:

Through baptism and confirmation, make him (her) your faithful follower and a witness to your gospel. Lord, hear us.

All: **Lord, graciously hear us.**

Reader:

Lead him (her) by a holy life to the joys of God's kingdom. Lord, hear us.

All: **Lord, graciously hear us.**

Reader:

MAKE the lives of his (her) parents and godparents examples of faith to inspire this child. Lord, hear us.

All: **Lord, graciously hear us.**

Reader:
Keep his (her) family always in your love. Lord, hear us.

All: **Lord, graciously hear us.**

Reader:
RENEW the grace of our baptism in each one of us. Lord, hear us.

All: **Lord, graciously hear us.**

The celebrant next invites all present to invoke the saints.

Holy Mary, Mother of God, **pray for us.**
Saint John the Baptist, **pray for us.**
Saint Joseph, **pray for us.**
Saint Peter and Saint Paul, **pray for us.**

The names of other saints may be added.

The litany concludes:
All holy men and women, pray for us.

PRAYER OF EXORCISM AND ANOINTING BEFORE BAPTISM

After the invocation, the celebrant says:

Almighty and ever-living God, ✤ you sent your only Son into the world ✤ to cast out the power of Satan, spirit of evil, ✤ to rescue man from the kingdom of darkness, ✤ and bring him into the splendour of your kingdom of light. ✤ We pray for this child: ✤ set him (her) free from original sin, ✤ make him (her) a temple of your glory, ✤ and send your Holy Spirit to dwell with him (her). ✤ (We ask this) through Christ our Lord.

All: **Amen.**

The celebrant continues:

We anoint you with the oil of salvation ✤ in the name of Christ our Saviour; ✤ may he strengthen you ✤ with his power, ✤ who lives and reigns for ever and ever.

All: **Amen.**

He anoints the child on the breast with the oil of catechumens.

CELEBRATION OF THE SACRAMENT

All proceed to the Baptistery. A hymn or psalm may be sung.

Celebrant:

My dear brothers and sisters, we now ask God to give this child new life in abundance through water and the Holy Spirit.

BLESSING AND INVOCATION OF GOD OVER BAPTISMAL WATER

(Other forms of this blessing may be used)

Celebrant:

PRAISE to you, almighty God and Father, for you have created water to cleanse and to give life.

All: **Blessed be God.**

Celebrant:

PRAISE to you, Lord Jesus Christ, the Father's only Son, for you offered yourself on the cross, that in the blood and water flowing from your side, and through your death and resurrection, the Church might be born.

Celebrant:

PRAISE to you, God the Holy Spirit, for you anointed Christ at his baptism in the waters of Jordan, so that we might all be baptized into you.

All: **Blessed be God.**

Celebrant:

COME to us, Lord, Father of all, and make holy this water which you have created, so that all who are baptized in it may be washed clean of sin and be born again to live as your children.

All: **Hear us, Lord.**

Celebrant:

MAKE this water holy, Lord, so that all who are baptized into Christ's death and resurrection by this water may become more perfectly like your Son.

All: **Hear us, Lord.**

The celebrant touches the water with his right hand and continues:

Lord, make holy this water which you have created, so that all those whom you have chosen may be born again by the power of the Holy Spirit, and may take their place among your holy people.

All: **Hear us, Lord.**

If the baptismal water has already been blessed, the celebrant omits the invocation Come to us, Lord *and those which follow it, and says:*

You have called your child, N, to this cleansing water that he (she) may share in the faith of your Church and have eternal life. By the mystery of this consecrated water lead him (her) to a new and spiritual birth. (We ask this) through Christ our Lord.

All: **Amen.**

RENUNCIATION OF SIN AND PROFESSION OF FAITH

Celebrant:

Dear parents and godparents: You have come here to present this child for baptism. By water and the Holy Spirit he (she) is to receive the gift of new life from God, who is love.

On your part, you must make it your constant care to bring him (her) up in the practice of the faith. See that the divine life which God gives him (her) is kept safe from the poison of sin, to grow always stronger in his (her) heart.

If your faith makes you ready to accept this responsibility, renew now the vows of your own baptism. Reject sin; profess your faith in Christ Jesus. This is the faith of the Church. This is the faith in which this child is about to be baptized.

The celebrant questions the parents and godparents:

Celebrant: Do you reject Satan?

Parents and Godparents: **I do.**

Celebrant: And all his works?
Parents and Godparents: **I do.**

Celebrant: And all his empty promises?
Parents and Godparents: **I do.**

Next the celebrant asks for the threefold profession of faith from the parents and godparents:

Do you believe in God, the Father almighty, creator of heaven and earth?

Parents and Godparents: **I do.**

Celebrant:

Do you believe in Jesus Christ, his only Son, our Lord, who was born of the Virgin Mary, was crucified, died, and was buried, rose from the dead, and is now seated at the right hand of the Father?

Parents and Godparents: **I do.**

Celebrant:

Do you believe in the Holy Spirit, the holy catholic Church, the communion of saints, the forgiveness of sins, the resurrection of the body, and life everlasting?

Parents and Godparents: **I do.**

Celebrant:

THIS is our faith. This is the faith of the Church. We are proud to profess it, in Christ Jesus our Lord.

All: **Amen.**

BAPTISM

The celebrant invites the family to the font and questions the parents and godparents:

Celebrant:

Is it your will that N. should be baptized in the faith of the Church, which we have all professed with you?

Parents and Godparents: **It is.**

He baptizes the child, saying:
N. I BAPTIZE you in the name of the Father,

He immerses the child or pours water upon it.
and of the Son,

He immerses the child or pours water upon it a second time.
and of the Holy Spirit.

He immerses the child or pours water upon it a third time.

ANOINTING WITH CHRISM

Then the celebrant says:

GOD the Father of our Lord Jesus Christ has freed you from sin, given you a new birth by water and the Holy Spirit, and welcomed you into his holy people. He now anoints you with the chrism of salvation. As Christ was anointed Priest, Prophet, and King, so may you live always as a member of his body, sharing everlasting life.

All: **Amen.**

Then the celebrant anoints the child on the crown of the head with the sacred chrism, in silence.

CLOTHING WITH THE WHITE GARMENT

Celebrant:

N. YOU have become a new creation, and have clothed yourself in Christ. See in this white garment the outward sign of your Christian dignity. With your family and friends to help you by word and example, bring that dignity unstained into the everlasting life of heaven.

All: **Amen.**

The white garment is put on the child.

THE LIGHTED CANDLE

The celebrant takes the Easter candle and says:
Receive the light of Christ.

Someone from the family (such as the father or godfather) lights the child's candle from the Easter candle. The celebrant then says:

PARENTS and godparents, this light is entrusted to you to be kept burning brightly. This child of yours has been enlightened by Christ. He (she) is to walk always as a child of the light. May he (she) keep the flame of faith alive in his (her) heart. When the Lord comes, may he (she) go out to meet him with all the saints in the heavenly kingdom.

[*The* Ephphetha (Prayer over Ears and Mouth) *may now follow. The celebrant touches the ears and mouth of the child with his thumb, saying:*

THE Lord Jesus made the deaf hear and the dumb speak. May he soon touch your ears to receive his word, and your mouth to proclaim his faith, to the praise and glory of God the Father.

All: **Amen.**]

CONCLUSION OF THE RITE

✠

Next there is a procession to the altar, unless the baptism was performed in the sanctuary. The lighted candle is carried for the child.

✠

The following or an appropriate hymn may be sung.

> **You have put on Christ,
> in him you have been baptized.
> Alleluia, alleluia.**

✠

THE LORD'S PRAYER

✠

The celebrant stands in front of the altar and addresses the parents, godparents, and the whole assembly in these or similar words:

DEARLY beloved, this child has been reborn in baptism. He (she) is now called the child of God, for so indeed he (she) is. In confirmation he (she) will receive the full-

ness of God's Spirit. In holy communion he (she) will share the banquet of Christ's sacrifice, calling God his (her) Father in the midst of the Church. In the name of this child, in the Spirit of our common sonship, let us pray together in the words our Lord has given us:

All present join the celebrant in singing or saying:

O UR Father, ✛ who art in heaven, ✛ hallowed be thy name. ✛ Thy kingdom come. ✛ Thy will be done on earth, as it is in heaven. ✛ Give us this day our daily bread. ✛ And forgive us our trespasses ✛ as we forgive those who trespass against us. ✛ And lead us not into temptation, ✛ but deliver us from evil.

THE BLESSING

The celebrant first blesses the mother, who holds the child in her arms, then the father, and lastly the entire assembly:

Celebrant:

G OD the Father, through his Son, the Virgin Mary's child, has brought joy to all Christian mothers, as they see the hope of eternal life shine on their children. May he bless the mother of this child. She now thanks God for the gift of her child. May she be one with him (her) in thanking him for ever in heaven, in Christ Jesus our Lord.

All: **Amen.**

Celebrant:

GOD is the giver of all life, human and divine. May he bless the father of this child. He and his wife will be the first teachers of their child in the ways of faith. May they be also the best of teachers, bearing witness to the faith by what they say and do, in Christ Jesus our Lord.

All: **Amen.**

Celebrant:

BY God's gift, through water and the Holy Spirit, we are reborn to everlasting life. In his goodness, may he continue to pour out his blessings upon these sons and daughters of his. May he make them always, wherever they may be, faithful members of his holy people. May he send his peace upon all who are gathered here, in Christ Jesus our Lord.

All: **Amen.**

Celebrant:

MAY almighty God, the Father, and the Son, ✢ and the Holy Spirit, bless you.

All: **Amen.**

ACKNOWLEDGEMENTS

The Order of Confirmation from *The Book of Common Prayer*, the rights of which are vested in the Crown, are reproduced by permission of the Crown Patentee, Cambridge University Press.

The Confirmation Service from *The Alternative Service Book 1980*, copyright © The Central Board of Finance of the Church of England, is reproduced with permission.

The Rite of Confirmation outside Mass in the Catholic Church: Excerpts from the English translation of *Rite of Confirmation*; Second Edition © 1975, ICEL. All rights reserved.

The ORDER of CONFIRMATION from The BOOK of COMMON PRAYER

OR LAYING ON OF HANDS UPON THOSE THAT ARE BAPTIZED AND COME TO YEARS OF DISCRETION

Upon the day appointed, all that are to be then confirmed, being placed, and standing in order, before the Bishop; he (or some other Minister appointed by him) shall read this Preface following.

To the end that Confirmation may be ministered to the more edifying of such as shall receive it, the Church hath thought good to order, That none hereafter shall be Confirmed, but such as can say the Creed, the Lord's Prayer, and the Ten Commandments; and can also answer to such other Questions, as in the short Catechism are contained: which order is very convenient to be observed; to the end, that children, being now come to the years of discretion, and having learned what their Godfathers and Godmothers promised for them in Baptism, they may themselves, with their own mouth and consent, openly before the Church, ratify and confirm the same; and also promise, that by the grace of God they will evermore endeavour themselves faithfully to observe such things, as they, by their own confession, have assented unto.

Then shall the Bishop say,

Do ye here, in the presence of God, and of this congregation, renew the solemn promise and vow that was made in your name at your Baptism; ratifying and confirming the same in your own persons, and acknowledging yourselves bound to believe, and to do, all those things, which your Godfathers and Godmothers then undertook for you?

And every one shall audibly answer,
I do.

The Bishop.
OUR help is in the Name of the Lord;
 Answer. Who hath made heaven and earth.
 Bishop. Blessed be the Name of the Lord;
 Answer. Henceforth, world without end.
 Bishop. Lord, hear our prayers.
 Answer. And let our cry come unto thee.

The Bishop.
Let us pray.

✠

ALMIGHTY and everliving God, who hast vouchsafed to regenerate these thy servants by Water and the Holy Ghost, and hast given unto them forgiveness of all their sins: Strengthen them, we beseech thee, O Lord, with the Holy Ghost the Comforter, and daily increase in them thy manifold gifts of grace; the spirit of wisdom and understanding; the spirit of counsel and ghostly strength; the spirit of knowledge and true godliness; and fill them, O Lord, with the spirit of thy holy fear, now and for ever. *Amen.*

Then all of them in order kneeling before the Bishop, he shall lay his hand upon the head of every one severally, saying,

Defend, O Lord, this thy Child [or *this thy Servant*] with thy heavenly grace, that *he* may continue thine for ever; and daily increase in thy Holy Spirit more and more, until *he* come unto thy everlasting kingdom. Amen.

Then shall the Bishop say,
The Lord be with you.
Answer. And with thy spirit.

And (all kneeling down) the Bishop shall add,
Let us pray.

Our Father, which art in heaven, Hallowed be thy Name. Thy kingdom come. Thy will be done, in earth as it is in heaven. Give us this day our daily bread. And forgive us our trespasses, As we forgive them that trespass against us. And lead us not into temptation; But deliver us from evil. Amen.

And this Collect.

ALMIGHTY and everliving God, who makest us both to will and to do those things that be good and acceptable unto thy divine Majesty; We make our humble supplications unto thee for these thy servants, upon whom (after the example of thy holy Apostles) we have now laid our hands, to certify them (by this sign) of thy favour and gracious goodness towards them. Let thy fatherly hand, we beseech thee, ever be over them, let thy Holy Spirit ever be with them; and so lead them in the knowledge and obedience of thy Word, that in the end they may obtain everlasting life; through our Lord Jesus Christ, who with thee and the Holy Ghost liveth and reigneth, ever one God, world without end. *Amen.*

O ALMIGHTY Lord, and everlasting God, vouchsafe, we beseech thee, to direct, sanctify, and govern, both our hearts and bodies, in the ways of thy laws, and in the works of thy commandments; that, through thy most mighty protection both here and ever, we may be preserved in body and soul; through our Lord and Saviour Jesus Christ. *Amen.*

Then the Bishop shall bless them, saying thus,

THE Blessing of God Almighty, the Father, the Son, and the Holy Ghost, be upon you, and remain with you for ever. *Amen.*

And there shall none be admitted to the holy Communion, until such time as he be confirmed, or be ready and desirous to be confirmed.

The CONFIRMATION SERVICE *from* *The* ALTERNATIVE SERVICE BOOK

1980

THE PREPARATION

64 *At the entry of the ministers this, or another APPROPRIATE SENTENCE, may be used:*

> The Lord is my strength and my song,
> and has become my salvation. *Psalm 118.14*

and A HYMN, A CANTICLE or A PSALM may be sung.

65 *Bishop* The Lord be with you
All **and also with you.**

66 *If THE PRAYERS OF PENITENCE (Holy Communion Rite A sections 5-8) are to be used, they follow here.*

67 *Bishop*

Heavenly Father, by the power of your Holy Spirit you give to your faithful people new life in the water of baptism. Guide and strengthen us by that same Spirit, that we who are born again may serve you in faith and love, and grow into the full stature of your Son Jesus Christ, who is alive and reigns with you and the Holy Spirit, one God now and for ever. **Amen.**

THE MINISTRY OF THE WORD

68 *Sit*

If AN OLD TESTAMENT READING is to be read, one of the following may be chosen.

Joshua 24.14-24
Ezekiel 36.25a,26-28
Jeremiah 31.31-34

At the end the reader may say
This is the word of the Lord.

All
Thanks be to God.

Silence may be kept.

69 *A PSALM or A HYMN may be sung.*

70 *If A NEW TESTAMENT READING is to be read, one of the following may be chosen.*

1 Corinthians 12.12, 13
1 Peter 2.4-10
Galatians 5.16-25

At the end the reader may say
This is the word of the Lord.

All
Thanks be to God.

Silence may be kept.

71 A CANTICLE or A HYMN may be sung.

72 Stand
THE GOSPEL. When it is announced

All
Glory to Christ our Saviour.

One of the following may be chosen (see ASB pp. 271-273 [271, 272, and 273]).

Matthew 16.24-27
Luke 24.45-end
Mark 1.14-20
John 14.15-18

At the end the reader may say
This is the Gospel of Christ.

All
Praise to Christ our Lord.

Silence may be kept.

73 *Sit*

THE SERMON

At the end, silence may be kept.

74 *A HYMN may be sung.*

THE RENEWAL OF BAPTISMAL VOWS

75 *The candidates stand before the Bishop; he says*

You have come here to be confirmed. You stand in the presence of God and his Church. With your own mouth and from your own heart you must declare your allegiance to Christ and your rejection of all that is evil. Therefore I ask these questions:

Bishop Do you turn to Christ?
Answer **I turn to Christ.**

Bishop Do you repent of your sins?
Answer **I repent of my sins.**

Bishop Do you renounce evil?
Answer **I renounce evil.**

76 *Then the Bishop says*

You must now declare before God and his Church that you accept the Christian faith into which you were baptized, and in which you will live and grow.

Do you believe and trust in God the Father, who made the world?

Answer **I believe and trust in him.**

Bishop
Do you believe and trust in his Son Jesus Christ, who redeemed mankind?

Answer **I believe and trust in him.**

Bishop
Do you believe and trust in his Holy Spirit, who gives life to the people of God?

Answer **I believe and trust in him.**

77 *The Bishop turns to the congregation and says*

This is the faith of the Church.

All

This is our faith. We believe and trust in one God, Father, Son, and Holy Spirit.

THE CONFIRMATION

78 *The Bishop stands before those to be confirmed and says*

Our help is in the name of the Lord

All **who has made heaven and earth.**

Bishop Blessed be the name of the Lord

All **now and for ever. Amen.**

79 *The Bishop stretches out his hands towards them and says*

ALMIGHTY and everlasting God, you have given your *servants* new birth in baptism by water and the Spirit, and have forgiven *them* all *their* sins. Let your Holy Spirit rest upon *them*: the Spirit of wisdom and understanding; the Spirit of counsel and inward strength; the Spirit of knowledge and true godliness; and let *their* delight be in the fear of the Lord. **Amen.**

80 *The Bishop lays his hand on the head of each candidate, saying*
Confirm, O, Lord, your servant N with your Holy Spirit.

and each one answers
Amen.

81 *After confirmation, the Bishop invites the people to join with him and say*

Defend, O Lord, your *servants* with your heavenly grace, that *they* may continue yours for ever, and daily increase in your Holy Spirit more and more, until *they come* to your everlasting kingdom. **Amen.**

82 *If some members of the congregation are now to make a renewal of their baptismal vows, sections 94-98 may be used here.*

THE COMMUNION

83 *The Bishop resumes the Communion Service at* THE PEACE.

CONFIRMATION WITHOUT HOLY COMMUNION

After section 81, the Bishop says one or more of these prayers.

86 *For those who have now been confirmed*

Heavenly Father, we pray for your *servants* upon whom we have now laid our hands, after the example of the apostles, to assure *them* by this sign of your favour towards *them*. May your fatherly hand ever be over *them*, your Holy Spirit ever be with *them*. Strengthen *them* continually with the Body and Blood of your Son, and so lead *them* in the knowledge and obedience of your word, that in the end *they* may obtain everlasting life; through Jesus Christ our Lord. **Amen.**

87 *For all Christian people*

Almighty Father, we thank you for our fellowship in the household of faith with all those who have been baptized in your name. Keep us faithful to our baptism, and so make us ready for that day when the whole creation shall be made perfect in your Son, our Saviour Jesus Christ. **Amen.**

88 *For the Church's witness*

ALMIGHTY God, whose Holy Spirit equips the Church with a rich variety of gifts: grant that we may use them to bear witness to Christ by lives built on faith and love. Make us ready to live his Gospel and eager to do his will, that we may share with all your Church in the joys of eternal life; through Jesus Christ our Lord. **Amen.**

89

LORD, make us instruments of your peace. Where there is hatred, let us sow love; where there is injury, let there be pardon; where there is discord, union; where there is doubt, faith; where there is despair, hope; where there is darkness, light; where there is sadness, joy; for your mercy and for your truth's sake. **Amen.**

90

LORD Jesus Christ, we thank you for all the benefits you have won for us, for all the pains and insults you have borne for us. Most merciful redeemer, friend and brother, may we know you more clearly, love you more dearly, and follow you more nearly, day by day. **Amen.**

91

ETERNAL God, you have declared in Christ the completion of your purpose of love. May we live by faith, walk in hope, and be renewed in love, until the world reflects your glory, and you are all in all. Even so; come, Lord Jesus. **Amen.**

92 *Then all say THE LORD'S PRAYER.*

93 *The Bishop ends the service with A BLESSING.*

The RITE of CONFIRMATION OUTSIDE MASS in the CATHOLIC CHURCH

A PSALM or HYMN may be sung as the bishop and his ministers come to the altar.

The bishop greets the people:

Bishop: Peace be with you.
All: **And also with you.**

Bishop:
Let us pray.

GOD of power and mercy, send your Holy Spirit to live in our hearts and make us temples of his glory. We ask this through our Lord Jesus Christ, your Son, who lives and reigns with you and the Holy Spirit, one God, for ever and ever.

All:
Amen.

or one of the prayers may be said from the Confirmation Masses (pages 91-5)

CELEBRATION OF THE WORD OF GOD

The celebration of the Word of God follows. At least one of the readings suggested for the Mass of confirmation is read.

SACRAMENT OF CONFIRMATION

HOMILY

After the Gospel, those to be confirmed are called forward to the sanctuary, and the bishop gives a brief HOMILY in these or similar words:

On the day of Pentecost the apostles received the Holy Spirit as the Lord had promised. They also received the power of giving the Holy Spirit to others and so completing the work of baptism. This we read in the Acts of the Apostles. When Saint Paul placed his hands on those who had been baptized, the Holy Spirit came upon them, and they began to speak in other languages and in prophetic words.

Bishops are successors of the apostles and have this power of giving the Holy Spirit to the baptized, either personally or through the priests they appoint.

In our day the coming of the Holy Spirit in confirmation is no longer marked by the gift of tongues, but we know his coming by faith. He fills our hearts with the love of God, brings us together in one faith but in different vocations, and works within us to make the Church one and holy.

The gift of the Holy Spirit which you are to receive will be a spiritual sign and seal to make you more like Christ and more perfect members of his Church. At his baptism by John, Christ himself was anointed by the Spirit and sent out on his public ministry to set the world on fire.

You have already been baptized into Christ and now you will receive the power of his Spirit and the sign of the cross on your forehead. You must be witnesses before all the world to his suffering, death, and resurrection; your way of life should at all times reflect the goodness of Christ. Christ gives varied gifts to his Church, and the Spirit distributes them among the members of Christ's body to build up the holy people of God in unity and love.

Be active members of the Church, alive in Jesus Christ. Under the guidance of the Holy Spirit give your lives completely in the service of all, as did Christ, who came not to be served but to serve.

So now, before you receive the Spirit, I ask you to renew the profession of faith you made in baptism or your parents and godparents made in union with the whole Church.

RENEWAL OF BAPTISMAL PROMISES

All stand, and the Bishop questions the Confirmands, who all reply together

Bishop:

Do you reject Satan and all his works and all his empty promises?

Bishop:

Do you believe in God the Father almighty, creator of heaven and earth?

Bishop:

Do you believe in Jesus Christ, his only Son, our Lord, who was born of the Virgin Mary, was crucified, died, and was buried, rose from the dead, and is now seated at the right hand of the Father?

Confirmands: **I do.**

Bishop:

Do you believe in the Holy Spirit, the Lord, the giver of life, who came upon the apostles at Pentecost and today is given to you sacramentally in confirmation?

Confirmands: **I do.**

Bishop:

Do you believe in the holy catholic Church, the communion of saints, the forgiveness of sins, the resurrection of the body, and life everlasting?

Confirmands: **I do.**

A HYMN expressing faith may now be sung. Or the bishop accepts the confirmands' profession by proclaiming the Church's faith in these or similar words:

Bishop:

THIS is our faith. This is the faith of the Church. We are proud to profess it in Christ Jesus our Lord.

All the faithful assent by answering:

All:
Amen.

THE LAYING ON OF HANDS

The concelebrating priests stand near the bishop. He faces the people and with hands joined, sings or says:

Bishop:

MY dear friends: In baptism God our Father gave the new birth of eternal life to his chosen sons and daughters. Let us pray to our Father that he will pour out the Holy Spirit to strengthen his sons and daughters with his gifts and anoint them to be more like Christ the Son of God.

All pray in silence for a short time.

The bishop and the priests who will minister the sacrament with him lay hands upon all the candidates (by extending their hands over them). The bishop alone sings or says:

Bishop:

All-powerful God, Father of our Lord Jesus Christ, by water and the Holy Spirit you freed your sons and daughters from sin and gave them new life. Send your Holy Spirit upon them to be their Helper and Guide. Give them the spirit of wisdom and understanding, the spirit of right judgment and courage, the spirit of knowledge and reverence. Fill them with the spirit of wonder and awe in your presence. We ask this through Christ our Lord.

All:
Amen.

THE ANOINTING WITH CHRISM

The deacon brings the chrism to the bishop. Each candidate goes to the bishop, or the bishop may go to the individual candidates. The one who presented the candidate places his right hand on the latter's shoulder and gives the candidate's name to the bishop; or the candidate may give his own name.

The bishop dips his right thumb in the chrism and makes the sign of the cross on the forehead of the one to be confirmed, as he says:

Bishop:
N., be sealed with the Gift of the Holy Spirit.

Confirmand:
Amen.

Bishop:
Peace be with you.

Confirmand:
And also with you.

If priests assist the bishop in conferring the sacrament, all the vessels of chrism are brought to the bishop by the deacon or by other ministers. Each of the priests comes to the bishop, who gives him a vessel of chrism.

The candidates go to the bishop or to the priests, or the bishop and priests may go to the candidates. The anointing is done as described above.

During the anointing a suitable song may be sung. After the anointing the bishop and the priests wash their hands.

GENERAL INTERCESSIONS

The general intercessions follow, in this or a similar form determined by the competent authority.

Bishop:

My dear friends: let us be one in prayer to God our Father as we are one in the faith, hope, and love his Spirit gives.

The deacon or minister reads the invocations:

Deacon/Minister:

For these sons and daughters of God, confirmed by the gift of the Spirit, that they give witness to Christ by lives built on faith and love: Lord, hear us.

All:
Lord, graciously hear us.

Deacon/Minister:

For their parents and godparents who led them in faith, that by word and example they may always encourage them to follow the way of Jesus Christ: Lord, hear us.

All:
Lord, graciously hear us.

Deacon/Minister:

For the holy Church of God, in union with N. our pope, N. our bishop, and all the bishops, that God, who gathers us together by the Holy Spirit, may help us grow in unity of faith and love until his Son returns in glory: Lord, hear us.

All:
Lord, graciously hear us.

Deacon/Minister:

For all men, of every race and nation, that they may acknowledge the one God as Father, and in the bond of common brotherhood seek his kingdom, which is peace and joy in the Holy Spirit: Lord, hear us.

All:
Lord, graciously hear us.

Deacon/Minister:

God our Father, you sent your Holy Spirit upon the apostles and through them and their successors you give the Spirit to your people. May his work begun at Pentecost continue to grow in the hearts of all who believe. We ask this through Christ our Lord.

All:
Amen.

The bishop introduces the OUR FATHER in these or similar words:

Bishop:
Dear friends in Christ, let us pray together as the Lord Jesus Christ has taught.

All:
Our Father . . .

BLESSING OR PRAYER

The BLESSING or PRAYER OVER THE PEOPLE follows:

1. BLESSING

Bishop:

GOD our Father made you his children by water and the Holy Spirit: may he bless you and watch over you with his fatherly love.

All:
Amen.

Bishop:

JESUS Christ the Son of God promised that the Spirit of truth would be with his Church for ever: may he bless you and give you courage in professing the true faith.

All:
Amen.

Bishop:

THE Holy Spirit came down upon the disciples and set their hearts on fire with love: may he bless you, keep you one in faith and love and bring you to the joy of God's kingdom.

All:
Amen.

Bishop:

MAY almighty God bless you, the Father, and the Son, ✠ and the Holy Spirit.

All:
Amen.

2. PRAYER OVER THE PEOPLE

The deacon or minister invites the people in words such as:

Deacon/Minister:
Bow your heads and pray for God's blessing.

Bishop:

GOD our Father, complete the work you have begun and keep the gifts of your Holy Spirit active in the hearts of your people. Make them ready to live his Gospel and eager to do his will. May they never be ashamed to proclaim to all the world Christ crucified living and reigning for ever and ever.

All:
Amen.

Bishop:
And may the blessing of almighty God, the Father, and the Son, ✢ and the Holy Spirit, come upon you and remain with you for ever.

All:
Amen.

CONFIRMATION MASSES

(not for use on Sundays of Advent, Lent or Easter, or other Solemnities, nor may they be said on Ash Wednesday or during Holy Week).

MASS NO. 1

ENTRY ANTIPHON (EX. 36, 25-26)

I will pour clean water on you and I will give you a new heart, a new spirit within you, says the Lord.

COLLECT

1. GOD of power and mercy, send your Holy Spirit to live in our hearts and make us temples of his glory. We ask this through our Lord Jesus Christ . . .

or

2. LORD, fulfill your promise. Send your Holy Spirit to make us witnesses before the world to the good news proclaimed by Jesus Christ our Lord, who lives and reigns . . .

or

3. LORD, fulfill the promise given by your Son and send the Holy Spirit to enlighten our minds and lead us to all truth. Grant this through our Lord Jesus Christ . . .

or

4. LORD, send us your Holy Spirit to help us walk in unity of faith and grow in the strength of his love to the full stature of Christ, who lives and reigns . . .

PRAYER OVER THE OFFERINGS

Lord, we celebrate the memorial of our redemption by which your Son won for us the gift of the Holy Spirit. Accept our offerings, and send us your Holy Spirit to make us more like Christ in bearing witness to the world. We ask this through Christ our Lord.

HANC IGITUR

(for use with the Roman Canon)

Father, accept this offering from your whole family and from those reborn in baptism and confirmed by the coming of the Holy Spirit. Protect them with your love and keep them close to you. (Through Christ our Lord. Amen.)

COMMUNION ANTIPHON (CF HEB. 6-4)

All you have been enlightened, who have experienced the gift of heaven and who have received your share of the Holy Spirit: rejoice in the Lord.

POST-COMMUNION

Lord, help those you have anointed by your Spirit and fed with the body and blood of your Son. Support them through every trial and by their works of love build up the Church in holiness and joy. Grant this through Christ our Lord.

MASS NO. 2

ENTRY ANTIPHON (ROM. 5: 5, 8: 11)

✜

THE love of God has been poured into our hearts by his Spirit living in us.

✜

COLLECT

LORD, send us your Holy Spirit to help us walk in unity of faith and grow in the strength of his love to the full stature of Christ, who lives and reigns with you and the Holy Spirit, one God, for ever and ever.

(other prayers from Mass No. 1 may be chosen)

PRAYER OVER THE OFFERINGS

Lord, you have signed our brothers and sisters with the cross of your Son and anointed them with the oil of salvation. As they offer themselves with Christ, continue to fill their hearts with your Spirit. We ask this through Christ our Lord.

HANC IGITUR
(as Mass I for Roman Canon)

COMMUNION ANTIPHON (PS. 33: 6, 9)

Look up at him with gladness and smile; taste and see the goodness of the Lord.

POST-COMMUNION

Lord, you give your Son as food to those you anoint with your Spirit. Help them to fulfill your law by living in freedom as your children. May they live in holiness and be your witnesses to the world. We ask this through Christ our Lord.

PICTURE CREDITS

The following illustrations come from manuscripts in the Bodleian Library, Oxford: Auct D. inf.2.11 f.93v (216); Canon Bib. Lat. 62, f.3 (15, 87); f.12v (1, 87); f.25v (12, 26, 57, 66, 79, 91); Canon Liturg. 178 f.104 (90); Canon Liturg. 378 f.119v (94); Corpus Christi 410 f.2v (62); f.5v (3, 8, 19, 33, 40, 55, 61, 75); f.11 (11); f.20v (70, 84); f.32 (59); f.36v (89); Douce 112 f.21 (2 and front cover); Douce 311 f.14v (78); f.122 (68); Laud Mis. 740 f.25v (10); Lat. th. b.4 f.101 (5, 24, 28, 64); Liturg. 41 f.110 (56, 83); New College 65 f.77 (92); Queens 349 f.36v (39); Rawl. A 417 f.37v (63) E.T.Archive (81); Giraudon (43, 77); Scala (22, 24, 30)